D1607980

The Greatest Choruses, Praise Songs, and Contemporary Artist Favorites

Compiled by Dennis Allen

Arranged by Dennis Allen, Steven V. Taylor, and Tom Fettke

WORDS ONLY

Lillenas PUBLISHING COMPANY

KANSAS CITY, MO 64141

Songs for Youth

1
Shine

Words by Steve Taylor
Music by Peter Furler

Shine, make 'em wonder
    what you got,
Make 'em wish that they were not
    on the outside looking bored.
Shine, let it shine before all men,
Let 'em see good works and then
    let 'em glorify the Lord.

2
Ask, Seek, Knock

Words by Paul Baloche
Music by Ed Kerr

Ask and it will be given to you.
Seek and you will find.
Knock and the door
    will be opened to you,
The door will be opened to you.

For everyone who asks, receives.
He who seeks, will find
And to him who knocks
    the door will be opened,
The door will be opened.

3
Willing Heart

by David E. Bell

Lord, give me a willing heart,
Lord, give me a brand new start.
Create in me a love that's real,
Give me a willing heart.
(Sing again)

4
I Pledge Allegiance to the Lamb

by Ray Boltz

I pledge allegiance to the Lamb
With all my strength, with all I am.
I will seek to honor His command,
I pledge allegiance to the Lamb.

5
Big House

*by Mark Stuart, Barry Blair,
Will McGinniss and Bob Herdman*

1. I don't know where
    you lay your head
    or where you call your home.
  I don't know where
    you eat your meals or
    where you talk on the phone.
  I don't know if you got a cook,
    a butler or a maid.
  I don't know if you got a yard
    with a hammock in the shade.

2. I don't know
    if you got some shelter
    or say a place to hide.
  I don't know if you live with friends
    in whom you can confide.

I don't know if you got a family,
  say a mom or dad.
I don't know if you feel love at all
  but I bet you wish you had.

Chorus:
  Come and go with me
    to my Father's house;
  Come and go with me
    to my Father's house.
  It's a big, big house
    with lots and lots of rooms,
  A big, big table
    with lots and lots of food.
  It's a big, big yard
    where we can play *football,*
  A big, big house,
    it's my Father's house!

3. All I know is a big ole house
    with rooms for everyone.
  All I know is lots of land
    where we can play and run.
  All I know is you need love
    and I've got a family.
  All I know is you're all alone
    so why not come with me?
  (Chorus again)

6
Change My Heart, O God

by Eddie Espinosa

Change my heart, O God,
  make it ever true;
Change my heart, O God,
  may I be like You.
You are the Potter, I am the clay;
Mold me and make me,
  this is what I pray.

Change my heart, O God,
  make it ever true;
Change my heart, O God,
  may I be like You.

7
I'm Not Ashamed

*Words by Peter Furler
and Steve Taylor
Music by Peter Furler*

Chorus:
  I'm not ashamed to let you know
  I want this light in me to show.
  I'm not ashamed to speak
    the name of Jesus Christ.

1. What are we sneaking around for?
  Who are we tryin' to please?
  Shrugging off sin, apologizing
  Like we're spreadin' some kinda
    disease,
  I'm saying, "No way. (No way.)
    No way. (No way.")
  (Chorus again)

2. This one says it's a lost cause,
  Save your testimonies for
    churchtime.
  The other ones state,
    "You better wait
  Until you do a little
    market research."
  I'm saying, "No way. *(No way.)*
    No way. *(No way.")*
  (Chorus again)

8
Lord, I Lift Your Name on High

by Rick Founds

Lord, I lift Your name on high.
Lord, I love to sing Your praises.
I'm so glad You're in my life.
I'm so glad You came to save us.

You came from heaven to earth
  to show the way,
From the earth to the cross,
  my debt to pay.
From the cross to the grave,
  from the grave to the sky,
Lord, I lift Your name on high!

9
Here Is My Heart

by Jonathan Wolfe

Jesus, I love You.
I lay my life before You.
I want to know You.
Here is my heart.

10
Stuff of Heaven

by Jeffery B. Scott

1. I used to like to dream
       that I'd be rich
       beyond compare.
   I'd never have a worry
       in the world,
   I'd never have a care.
   But now I know
       those things are useless,
       causing worry and pain.
   The one true wealth
       I've got to follow
       is the power of Jesus' name.

Chorus:
   See fame and glory
       don't count much
       in the Father's eyes,
   Or seeking objects made of gold.
   The only things that matter
       are faith, hope, and love.
   The stuff of heaven
       will never grow old.

2. We measure our successes
       by all the things we've got.
   Whoever has the most toys
       wins in the end, least that's
       what we've been taught.
   But all that stuff don't really matter,
       it's just rust and decay,
   And when we get to heaven
       we can't keep 'em anyway.
(Chorus again)

11
Seek First

by Amy Grant and Wes King

Chorus:
Seek first the kingdom of heaven
       and all shall be added.
Seek first the kingdom of heaven
       and all shall be added.

Verse:
They say we need money and power
They say there's no God up above.
Don't they know our Friend in high
       places?
Nothing can be stronger than love.
   (Chorus again)

12
God Is Gonna Finish
Just What He Started

by Morris Chapman

Chorus:
God is gonna finish
       just what He started
Even though the waters
       got to be parted.
Lift up your heads;
       don't be brokenhearted.
God is gonna finish
       what He started in you.
(Chorus again)

Verse:
He who began a good work in you
       is able to complete it.
He who began a good work in you
       is able to complete it.
(Chorus again)

13
I Love You, Lord

by Laurie Klein

I love You, Lord, and I lift my voice
To worship You. O my soul, rejoice!
Take joy, my King, in what You hear;
May it be a sweet, sweet sound
    in Your ear.

14
I Will Lift High

by Dan Whittemore

I will lift high the Lord God at all times.
I will sing His praise
    the rest of my years.
I sought the Lord
    and He graciously answered.
He took away from me
    my greatest fear.
He took away from me
    my greatest fear.

For the eye of the Lord is upon me;
His ear is attentive to my every cry.
His face shines upon me;
    His strong arm surrounds me.
By grace He has saved me
    and I'll never die.

15
We Are Standing

author unknown

I am standing for Jesus,
I am standing for Him.

Wherever I may go
    I want the world to know
That I am standing for Him.

Optional Chorus:
We are standing for Jesus,
We are standing for Him.
Wherever I may go
    I want the world to know
That we are standing for Him.

16
You Are My All in All

by Dennis Jernigan

1. You are my strength
        when I am weak,
    You are the treasure that I seek.
    You are my all in all.
    Seeking You as a precious jewel,
    Lord, to give up, I'd be a fool.
    You are my all in all.

Chorus:
    Jesus, Lamb of God,
    Worthy is Your name.
    Jesus, Lamb of God,
    Worthy is Your name.

2. Taking my sin, my cross, my shame.
    Rising again, I bless Your name.
    You are my all in all.
    When I fall down, You pick me up.
    When I am dry, You fill my cup.
    You are my all in all.
    (Chorus again)

17
Pharaoh, Pharaoh

by Tony Sbrano

Chorus:
    Pharoah, Pharoah, oh, baby,
    Let my people go. *Uh!*
    Yeah, yeah, yeah, yeah, I said:
    Pharoah, Pharoah, oh, baby,
    Let my people go. *Uh!*
    Yeah, yeah, yeah, yeah.

1. Well a burnin' bush told me
        the other day
   That I should come over here
        and stay
   Gotta get my people outta
        Pharaoh's hand
   And lead them all
        to the promised land. I said:
   (Chorus again)

2. Well, a-me 'n God's people
        comin' to the Red Sea,
   And Pharaoh's army
        comin' after me.
   I raised my rod
        and stuck it in the sand
   And all of God's people walked
        across the dry land. I said:
   (Chorus again)

3. Well, a Pharaoh's army
        is a comin' too,
   So what do you think that I did do?
   I raised my rod
        and I cleared my throat
   And all of Pharaoh's army did the
        "dead man float." I said:
   (Chorus 2 times)

   I said: Pharoah, Pharoah, oh, baby,
   Let my people go. *Uh!*

18
Be Bold, Be Strong

by Morris Chapman

Be bold, *(Be bold,)*
    be strong, *(be strong,)*
For the Lord your God is with you.
Be bold, *(Be bold,)*
    be strong, *(be strong,)*
For the Lord your God is with you.

I am not afraid;
I am not dismayed,
'Cause I'm walkin' in faith
    and victory.
Come on and walk in faith
    and victory,
For the Lord your God is with you.

19
Jesus, You Alone Are Worthy*
with
Worship You in Spirit**

* by Jennifer Randolph
** by Danny Chambers

*Jesus, You alone are worthy
    and I lift my voice to You.
Jesus, You alone are worthy.
I will worship none but You.
(Sing again)

**I will worship You in spirit,
I will worship You in truth.
I will worship You
    with my whole heart.
I will worship You in all I say and do.

20
O Lord, My Rock

by Cathy Jeffers Risse

O Lord, my Rock and my Redeemer,
You are a holy God
    and clothed in righteousness!
O Lord, my Rock and my Redeemer,
Let my life be an offering unto You.

21
I Believe

Words by Wes and Fran King
Music by Wes King

1. I believe in six days and a rest.
   God is good, I do confess.
   I believe in Adam and Eve,
   In a tree and a garden,
      in a snake and a thief.

Chorus:
   I believe, I believe,
   I believe in the Word of God.
   I believe, I believe,
   'Cause He made me believe.

2. I believe Isaiah
      was a prophet of old.
   The Lamb was slain
      just as He foretold.
   I believe Jesus was
      the Word made man,
   And He died for my sins,
      and He rose again.
(Chorus again)

22
In the Presence

by Mark Altrogge

And I cry, "Holy, holy, holy God.
How awesome is Your name!
Holy, holy, holy God.
How majestic is Your name!"
And I am changed
    in the presence of a holy God.

23
If God Is for Us

by Eddie DeGarmo
and Dana Key

If God is for us,
    who can be against us?
No power on earth
    can take His love away.
If God is for us,
    who can be against us?
We can live in victory today!

24
Let Me Love You

Words by Ken Bible
Music by Steven V. Taylor

My Father, let me love You,
    love You, love You
From a heart that's open
    and list'ning for Your voice.
Let me love You, truly love You,
    simply love You, loving Lord.

25
Celebrate Jesus

by Gary Oliver

Celebrate Jesus, celebrate,
Celebrate Jesus, celebrate.
Celebrate Jesus, celebrate,
Celebrate Jesus, celebrate.

He is risen, He is risen,
And He lives forevermore;
He is risen, He is risen,
Come on and celebrate
      the resurrection of our Lord.

26
Jesus Is a River of Love

by Dallas Holm

Well, my Jesus is a river of love,
And it flows from heaven above.
Take every sin you have
And He'll wash it away!

You gotta jump in the water today,
'Cause you won't drown
    if you learn to pray.
Well, my Jesus is a river of love
And He's flowin' your way!

27
Trust in the Lord

Words adapted from Prov. 3:5-6
Music by Dennis and Nan Allen

Trust in the Lord
    (Trust in the Lord)
    with all your heart

And lean not upon
    (and lean not upon)
    your own understanding.
In all your ways acknowledge Him
And He will direct your path,
And He will direct your path.

28
No Fear

by David Bell

There is no fear in Jesus Christ;
By His grace we're made new.
It's the cross that reminds me,
That in Him– no fear.

29
Not Ashamed

by Danny Chambers

Chorus:
We're not ashamed
    of the gospel of Christ. *No!*
His Word is power to save us.
We will declare
    He's the giver of life. *Yeah!*
Forever we'll sing His praises.

1. Too long we've hidden
    the Truth in our hearts,
    Quietly absorbing fiery darts.
    Our day of silence has come
      to a close.
    We're gonna shout
      till the whole world knows.
    (Chorus again)

2. Declare to the nations:
    Our God reigns,
    And among heathen
      we will praise His name.

We're not afraid
of opinions of man.
We're rising up
and we're taking a stand.
(Chorus again)

Forever we'll sing His praises.
Forever we'll sing His praises.

30
All That I Need

by John Paul Trimble

1. My only hope is You,
My only hope is You.
From early in the morning
till late at night,
My only hope is You.

2. My only hope is You,
My only hope is You.
From early in the morning
till late at night,
My only hope is You.

3. My only peace is You,
My only peace is You.
From early in the morning
till late at night,
My only peace is You.

4. My only joy is You,
My only joy is You.
From early in the morning
till late at night,
My only joy is You.

5. All that I need is You,
All that I need is You.
From early in the morning
till late at night,
All that I need is You;
All that I need is You.

31
Stand Up and Shout

Author unknown
Arr. by Dennis Allen

1. Stand up and shout
if you love my Jesus. *Yeah!*
Stand up and shout
if you love my Lord. *Yeah!*
I want to know, yes, I want to know
if you love my Lord.

2. Stand up and shout
if you love my Jesus. *Yeah!*
Stand up and shout
if you love my Lord. *Yeah!*
I want to know, yes, I want to know
if you love my Lord.

3. Sit down and whisper
if you love my Jesus. *Yeah!*
Sit down and whisper
if you love my Lord. *Yeah!*
I want to know, yes, I want to know
if you love my Lord.

4. Stand up and shout
if you love my Jesus. *Yeah!*
Stand up and shout
if you love my Lord. *Yeah!*
I want to know, yes, I want to know
if you love my Lord.

32
Open Our Eyes

by Bob Cull

Open our eyes, Lord,
we want to see Jesus;
To reach out and touch Him,
and say that we love Him.
Open our ears, Lord,
and help us to listen;
Open our eyes, Lord,
we want to see Jesus.

33
Carry the Light

by Twila Paris

Carry the light, carry the light.
Go and tell the children
    they are precious in His sight.
Carry the light, carry the light.
Go and preach the gospel
    till there is no more night.
In the name of Jesus Christ,
    carry the light.
(Sing again)

Carry the light, the light.
Carry the light.

34
Be the One

*by Al Denson, Don Koch
and Dave Clark*

1. Will you be the one
        to answer to His call,
   And will you stand
        when those around you fall?
   Will you be the one
        to take His light
        into a darkened world?
   Tell me, will you be the one?

2. Yes, I'll be the one
        to answer to His call,
   And I will stand
        when those around me fall.
   Yes, I'll be the one
        to take His light
        into a darkened world.
   Oh, yes, I'll be the one.

   Yes, I'll be the one
        to take His light
        into a darkened world.

Oh, yes, I'll be the one.

35
Awesome God

by Rich Mullins

Our God is an awesome God;
He reigns from heaven above
With wisdom, power, and love.
Our God is an awesome God!
(Sing again)

Our God is an awesome God!
Our God is an awesome God!
Our God is an awesome God!

36
The Kingdom of
Our God Has Come

*Words by Ken Bible
Music by Randall Dennis*

Chorus:
O life and joy!
The kingdom of God has come!
O love and peace!
The kingdom of God has come!
In Jesus Christ
    His blessings have begun.
O the kingdom of
    our God has come!
Yes, the kingdom of
    our God has come!

1. The empty in spirit
        are filled with Him,
   And those who have mourned
        are glad again;
   The meek hold the riches
        of Christ within.

Yes, the kingdom of God
has come!
(Chorus again)

2. Are you hungry for holiness?
Come to Him!
Have you fallen?
Just trust again!
We sinners are pure
'cause our Lord's within.
Yes, the kingdom of God
has come!
(Chorus again)

Well, there's peace in our hearts,
perfect peace, and we'll share it.
Troubles may come,
but in Him we will bear it.
Joy is in Jesus! We have to declare:
The kingdom of God has come!
(Chorus again)

Yes, the kingdom of our God
has come!

37
Step by Step

by Beaker

O God, You are my God,
and I will ever praise You.
O God, You are my God,
and I will ever praise You.

I will seek You in the morning,
and I will learn to walk
in Your way;
And step by step You'll lead me,
and I will follow You
all of my days.

O God, You are my God,
and I will ever praise You.
O God, You are my God,
and I will ever praise You.

And step by step You'll lead me,
and I will follow You
all of my days.

38
I Want to Be a History Maker

by Graham Kendrick

1. I want to be a history maker.
(I want to be a history maker.)
I want to be a world shaker.
(I want to be a world shaker.)
To be a pen on history's pages,
(To be a pen on history's
pages,)
Faithful to the end of the ages.
(Faithful to the end of the
ages.)

Chorus:
I want to see Your kingdom come;
I want to see Your will be done
on the earth.
I want to see Your kingdom come;
I want to see Your will be done
on the earth as it is in heaven.

2. We want to be the generation,
(We want to be the
generation,)
Taking the news to every nation.
(Taking the news to every
nation.)
Filled with the Spirit
without measure,
(Filled with the Spirit without
measure,)
Working for a heavenly treasure.
(Working for a heavenly
treasure.)
(Chorus again)

I want to be a history maker.

39
Let Me See

by David Bell

Open my eyes, let me see.
Open my ears, let me hear.
Open my heart,
    let me love You, Jesus.
Open my eyes, let me see.
Open my ears, let me hear.
Open my heart, I love You.

40
Jesus Is the Rock

by Tony Congi

Jesus is a Rock
    and He rolls my blues away.
    Bop, she bop, she bop, wow!
Jesus is a Rock
    and He rolls my blues away.
    Bop, she bop, she bop, wow!
Jesus is a Rock
    and He rolls my blues away.
    Bop, she bop, she bop, wow!

Jesus is a Rock and He rolls my blues,
Jesus is a Rock and He rolls my blues
    away.

41
God Will Make a Way

by Don Moen

God will make a way
    where there seems to be no way.
He works in ways we can not see,
He will make a way for me.
He will be my guide,
    hold me closely to His side,
With love and strength
    for each new day,
He will make a way,
    He will make a way.

42
God Still Moves

by Chris Machen

God still moves, God still moves,
In the hearts of His people
    He still moves.
He does not sleep
    nor does He slumber.
God still moves, God still moves.

43
Jesus Is Lord
of the Way I Feel

by Don Francisco

Chorus:
Praise the Lord, Hallelu,
I don't care
    what the devil's gonna do!
The Word in faith
    is my sword and shield;
Jesus is the Lord of the way I feel.
    I say
(Sing again)

Verse:
O clap de hands, stomp de feet,
Spread the love of Jesus
    with everyone you meet!
O clap de hands, stomp de feet,
Spread a little love around!
    I say now
(Chorus again)

I feel, the way I feel.

44
Friends

by Michael W. Smith
and Deborah D. Smith

1. Packing up the dreams
    God planted
In the fertile soil of you;
Can't believe the hopes
    He's granted
Means a chapter in your life
    is through.
But we'll keep you close as always;
It won't even seem you've gone,
'Cause our hearts in big
    and small ways
Will keep the love
    that keeps us strong.

Chorus:
And friends are friends forever
    If the Lord's the Lord of them.
And a friend will not say "never"
    'Cause the welcome will not end,
Though it's hard to let you go,
    In the Father's hands we know
That a lifetime's not too long
    to live as friends.

2. With the faith and love
    God's given,
Springing from the hope we know,
We will pray the joy you'll live in
Is the strength that now you show.
But we'll keep you close as always;
It won't even seem you've gone,
'Cause our hearts in big
    and small ways
Will keep the love
    that keeps us strong.
(Chorus again)

45
Let My Life Be the Praise

by Dennis and Nan Allen

Let my life be the praise
    that raises You, Lord.
Let my life be the praise;
    Be glorified in all that I do,
As a daily reflection
    of Your godly perfection.
Let my life be the praise,
    Let my life be the praise to You!

46
For the Sake of the Call

by Steven Curtis Chapman

We will abandon it all
    for the sake of the call.
No other reason at all—
    for the sake of the call.
Wholly devoted to live and to die
    for the sake of the call.

47
From the Rising of the Sun

Author unknown
Arr. by Steven V. Taylor

From the rising of the sun
    to the going down of the same,
The name of the Lord
    shall be praised.
From the rising of the sun
    to the going down of the same,
The name of the Lord
    shall be praised.

So praise ye the Lord.
    Praise ye the Lord.
From the rising of the sun
    to the going down of the same,
The name of the Lord
    shall be praised.
The name of the Lord
    shall be praised.

48
What a Mighty God We Serve

Author unknown
Arr. by Keith Phillips

What a mighty God we serve.
What a mighty God we serve.
Angels bow before Him,
    heaven and earth adore Him;
What a mighty God we serve.

49
Victory Chant

by Joseph Vogels

1. Hail, Jesus, You're my King.
    (Hail, Jesus, You're my King.)
Your life frees me to sing.
    (Your life frees me to sing.)
I will praise you all my days.
    (I will praise you all my days.)
Perfect in all Your ways.
    (Perfect in all Your ways.)

2. Hail, Jesus, You're my Lord.
    (Hail, Jesus, You're my Lord.)
I will obey Your Word.
    (I will obey Your Word.)
I want to see Your kingdom come.
    (I want to see Your kingdom
    come.)
Not my will, but Yours be done.
    (Not my will, but Yours be
    done.)

3. Glory, glory to the Lamb.
    (Glory, glory to the Lamb.)
You take me into the land.
    (You take me into the land.)
We will conquer in Your name,
    (We will conquer in Your
    name,)
And proclaim that Jesus reigns,
    (And proclaim that Jesus
    reigns.)
And proclaim that Jesus reigns.

50
Lord, Be Glorified

by Bob Kilpatrick

1. In my life, Lord,
    be glorified, be glorified.
In my life, Lord,
    be glorified today.

2. In Your Church, Lord,
    be glorified, be glorified.
In Your Church, Lord,
    be glorified today.

3. In my life, Lord,
  be glorified, be glorified.
In my life, Lord,
  be glorified today.

51
I Believe in Jesus

by Danny Chambers,
Jillian Chambers & Trent Austin

1. When the fires rage
  and the heat is on
I won't bow down
  I'm standin' strong!
When darkness falls,
  my voice will rise
Against the tide
  of compromise.
I'll take it to the streets
  around the world,
A song of love and freedom.
Proclaim the creed He lives in me!

Chorus:
I believe in Jesus.
  I believe that He died for me.
I believe that He set me free!
  I believe in Jesus.
I believe that He rose again
  for the heart of ev'ry man.

2. When the pressure's on
  and friends are few
I'll risk it all and speak the truth.
When the lofty looks of idols fall
By faith in God I'll be walkin' tall.
I'll take it to the streets
  around the world,
A song of love and freedom.
Proclaim the creed He lives in me!
(Chorus again)

52
I Waited Patiently

by Danny Chambers

Chorus:
I waited patiently for the Lord
And He inclined to me
  and heard my cry.
He also brought me up
  out of a horrible pit,
  out of the miry clay,
And set my feet upon a rock,
  and established my steps.
He has put a new song in my mouth.
Praise to our God!
(Chorus again)

Verse:
Many will see it and fear
  and will trust in the Lord.
Many will see it and fear
  and will trust in the Lord.
(Chorus again)

53
Sing unto the Lord

by Russell Lowe

Sing unto the Lord,
  sing to Him a new song.
Sing unto the Lord,
  sing to Him a new song.
Sing unto the Lord,
  sing to Him a new song.
Sing unto the Lord,
  sing to Him a new song.

Sing unto the Lord a new song,
Play skillfully with a loud noise.
For the Word of the Lord is right
  and all His works are done
  in truth.
The earth is full of the goodness
  of the Lord.

54
Whatever He Wants

by David E. Bell and Rod Padgett

1. I don't have the strength
      to make it through the day.
   So, I close my eyes,
      all I can do is pray.
   Lord, help me to stand,
      give me the words to say,
   So they can see You
      as I go on my way.

Chorus:
   I can do whatever He wants
      me to do.
   (I can do whatever He wants
      me to do.)
   I can do whatever He wants
      me to do.
   (I can do whatever He wants
      me to do.)
   Filled with His power,
      He'll see us through,
      standing together,
   We'll do what He wants us to do.

2. The future's unclear
      and everything's hard to see.
   I'm facing the fear
      of what is inside of me.
   Lord, I call on You,
      You see me through each day.
   You give me the strength
      as I go on my way.
Chorus:
   I can do whatever He wants
      me to do.
   (I can do whatever He wants
      me to do.)
   I can do whatever He wants
      me to do.
   (I can do whatever He wants
      me to do.)
   Filled with His power,
      He'll see us through,
      standing together,
   We'll do what He wants us to do.

55
Praise Him, Raise Him

by Dan Carson

Well, you gotta praise Him, raise Him.
Get together now and sing it,
   shout it!
He's the reason that we're standin',
   jammin'!
He's the reason that ya
   put your hands together,
   five, six, seven, eight!
Everything that breathes, *uh,*
   come now praise the Lord!
(Sing again)

Everything that breathes, *uh,*
   come now praise the Lord!
Well, we're talkin' everything
   that breathes, *uh,*
   come now praise the Lord!

56
Pass It On

by Kurt Kaiser

1. It only takes a spark
      to get a fire going,
   And soon all those around
      can warm up in its glowing.
   That's how it is with God's love,
      once you've experienced it.
   You spread His love to everyone.
      You want to pass it on.

2. What a wondrous time is spring
      when all the trees are budding,
   The birds begin to sing,
      the flowers start their blooming.
   That's how it is with God's love,
      once you've experienced it.
   You want to sing,
      it's fresh like spring.
      You want to pass it on.

3. I wish for you my friend
  this happiness that I've found.
You can depend on Him,
  it matters not where you're
  bound.
I'll shout it from the mountain top,
  I want my world to know.
The Lord of Love has come to me.
  I want to pass it on.

57
I Give All to You

by Larnelle Harris

I give all my *service to You.
I give all my service to You.
No matter the cost
  or what others do,
I give all my service to You.

Additional verses: problems, family, future, worship.

58
I Am Somebody

by Al Holley

I am somebody
  because God loves me,
And I'm accepted
  just the way that I am.
His love is higher;
  it's deeper and wider,
Than you and I will
  ever understand.

59
Only You

*Words by Ken Bible
Music by Steven V. Taylor*

All my hope, all my joy—
  only You.
Now forever, every moment—
  only You.
In each word, in each deed,
  not myself, not my strength,
Only You, Living Christ, only You.
(Sing again)

In each word, in each deed,
  not myself, not my strength,
Only You, Living Christ, only You.

60
Lean on Me

by Bill Withers

Chorus:
Lean on me
  when you're not strong,
And I'll be your friend;
  I'll help you carry on,
For it won't be long
  till I'm gonna need
  somebody to lean on.

I just might have a problem
  that you'll understand.
We all need somebody to lean on.
You just call on me, brother,
  when you need a hand.
We all need somebody to lean on.
(Chorus again)

61
You're the Reason We Sing

by Dan Carson

Jesus, we come to
    worship your name.
You alone are worthy,
    we crown you King of Kings.
Holy, holy, holy,
    let the praises ring.
You're the one we worship,
    You're the reason that we sing!
(Sing again)

Lord, we lift your holy name up high.
    (We lift your name up high.)
Lord, we welcome You,
    our special guest.
    (You are our special guest.)
Lord, we're here to sing
    our praise to You.
    (We sing our praise to You.)
You're the one,
    the reason that we sing!

Jesus, we come to
    worship your name.
You alone are worthy,
    we crown you King of Kings.
Holy, holy, holy,
    let the praises ring.
You're the one we worship,
    You're the reason that we sing!

You're the one we worship,
You're the reason
    that we sing!

62
Sing, Shout, Clap

by Billy Funk

Sing, shout, clap your hands;
    Give praise unto your Maker.

Make a joyful noise unto the Lord.
    Sing, shout, clap your hands;
Give praise unto your Maker,
    For the Lord, He is Almighty God.

This is the day of celebration;
    This is the day to rejoice! rejoice!
The Lord, our God, is our Deliverer,
    So let's just praise His name.

Sing, shout, clap your hands;
    Give praise unto your Maker.
Make a joyful noise unto the Lord.
    Sing, shout, clap your hands;
Give praise unto your Maker,
    For the Lord, He is Almighty God.

63
I Humble Myself Before You

by Bruce Wickersheim

I humble myself before You,
    falling down at Your feet;
I humble myself
    before the King of Kings.
And, worshipping at Your footstool,
    I offer my heart of praise;
In humbleness, Lord,
    I magnify Your name.

You are the Holy One;
    You are the Righteous Judge,
Creator of all life,
    and Sustainer of my soul.

I humble myself before You,
    falling down at Your feet;
I humble myself
    before the King of Kings.
And, worshipping at Your footstool,
    I offer my heart of praise;
In humbleness, Lord,
    I magnify Your name.

64
God's Not Dead

Author unknown
Arr. by Dennis Allen

God's not dead, *No!*
   He is alive!
God's not dead, *No!*
   He is alive!
God's not dead, *No!*
   He is alive!
I can feel Him in my hands;
God is alive!

God's not dead, *No!*
   He is alive!
God's not dead, *No!*
   He is alive!
God's not dead, *No!*
   He is alive!
I can feel Him in my feet;
   feel Him in my hands;
God is alive!

God's not dead, *No!*
   He is alive!
God's not dead, *No!*
   He is alive!
God's not dead, *No!*
   He is alive!
I can feel Him in my heart;
   feel Him in my feet;
   feel Him in my hands;
God is alive!

God's not dead, *No!*
   He is alive!
God's not dead, *No!*
   He is alive!
God's not dead, *No!*
   He is alive!
I can feel Him in my eyes;
   feel Him in my heart;
   feel Him in my feet;
   feel Him in my hands;
God is alive!

God's not dead, *No!*
   He is alive!
God's not dead, *No!*

He is alive!
God's not dead, *No!*
   He is alive!
I can feel Him in my soul;
   feel Him in my eyes;
   feel Him in my heart;
   feel Him in my feet;
   feel Him in my hands;
God is alive!

65
His Strength Is Perfect

by Steven Curtis Chapman
and Jerry Salley

Verse:
I can do all things
   thro' Christ who gives me
   strength,
But sometimes I wonder
   what He can do through me.
No great success to show,
   no glory on my own,
Yet in my weakness
   He is there to let me know–

Chorus:
His strength is perfect
   when our strength is gone.
He'll carry us
   when we can't carry on.
Raised in His power,
   the weak become strong.
His strength is perfect;
   His strength is perfect.
His strength is perfect;
   His strength is perfect.
(Chorus again)

Raised in His power,
   the weak become strong.
His strength is perfect;
   His strength is perfect.

66
You Are the One

by Keith and Melody Green

1. How I love you.
    You are the One,
    You are the One!
   How I love you.
    You are the One for me!

2. I was so lost,
    but You showed the way
    'cause You are the Way!
   I was so lost,
    but You showed the Way
    to me!

3. I was lied to,
    but You told the truth
    'cause You are the Truth!
   I was lied to,
    but You told the Truth to me!

4. I was dying,
    but You gave me life
    'cause You are the Life!
   I was dying,
    but You gave Your life for me!

You are the One,
God's risen Son,
You are the One for me.

67
Shine Out the Light

*by Dave Clark, Al Denson
and Don Koch*

Shine out the light, shine out the light;
    Shine out the light to the world.
Like a candle in the darkness
    burning through the night,
We've got to shine out the light
    to the world.

68
Hosanna, You're the King

by David Bell

Hosanna, You're the King,
    (Hosanna, You're the King,)
We worship and we sing.
    (We worship and we sing.)
We lift Your holy name
    (We lift Your holy name)
upon high!
    (upon high!)
We worship and adore,
    (We worship and adore,)
Give praise forevermore.
    (Give praise forevermore.)
Hosanna, You're the King,
    (Hosanna, You're the King,)
forevermore.
    (forevermore.)
(Sing again)

69
I've Got Something to Say

*by David Harris, Jeff Gunn
and Brian Tankersley*

Hey now, people,
    I've got something to say, singin',
"God's not dead. *No!*
    His children aren't ashamed."
Hey now, people,
    We're not just here to play.
Stand up, shout it!
    There's power in Jesus' name!
Hey now, people,
    I've got something to say.

70
Spring Up, O Well

Author unknown
Arr. by Steven V. Taylor

I've got a river of life
    flowing out of me–
Makes the lame to walk
    and the blind to see,
Opens prison doors,
    sets the captive free.
I've got a river of life
    flowing out of me.
Spring up, O well, within my soul.
Spring up, O well,
    and make me whole.
Spring up, O well, and give to me
    that life abundantly.

71
Shine, Jesus, Shine

by Graham Kendrick

Shine, Jesus, shine; fill this land
    with the Father's glory.
Blaze, Spirit, blaze;
    set our hearts on fire.
Flow, river, flow; flood the nations
    with grace and mercy.
Send forth Your Word,
    Lord, and let there be light.

72
The Blood of Jesus

Arr. by Dennis Allen

*O the Blood of Jesus
Author Unknown

**Nothing but the Blood
by Robert Lowry

***There Is Power in the Blood
by Lewis Jones

*O the blood of Jesus,
O the blood of Jesus,
O the blood of Jesus
    that washes white as snow.

**What can wash away my sin?
Nothing but the blood of Jesus.
What can make me whole again?
Nothing but the blood of Jesus.

O the blood of Jesus,
O the blood of Jesus,
O the blood of Jesus
    that washes white as snow.

***There is power, power,
    wonderworking power
In the blood of the Lamb.
There is power, power,
    wonderworking power
In the precious blood of the Lamb.

*O the blood of Jesus,
O the blood of Jesus,
O the blood of Jesus
    that washes white as snow.

73
I Will Stand

by Cliff Downs, Joel Lindsey,
Pamela Thum and Regie Hamm

In this world of temptation,
    I will stand for what is right.
With a heart of salvation,
    I will hold up the light.
If I live or if I die,
    if I laugh or if I cry,
In this world of temptation,
    I will stand.

74
I'm Yours

by Gary Chapman

Chorus:
I'm Yours, Lord; everything I've got,
    everything I am,
    everything I'm not.
I'm Yours, Lord;
    try me now and see,
see if I can be completely Yours.

1. My life and my love
        I leave in Your hands;
   I'll gladly perform
        as Your will demands.
   I know it's not much,
        Your gift to repay;
   But it's all I can give
        and all I can say is
(Chorus again)

2. You put in us all
        desire to belong,
   To join with Your strength
        and thus become strong.
   With that thought in mind,
        I reach for the prize;
   I lift up my voice
        to reemphasize that
(Chorus again)

See if I can be completely Yours.
See if I can be completely Yours.

75
He Will Carry You

by Scott Wesley Brown

There is no problem too big–
    God cannot solve it.
There is no mountain too tall–
    He cannot move it.
There is no storm too dark–
    God cannot calm it.

There is no sorrow too deep–
    He cannot soothe it.

Chorus:
If He carried the weight of the world
    upon His shoulder,
I know, my brother, that He
    will carry you.
If He carried the weight of the world
    upon His shoulder,
I know, my sister, that He
    will carry you.

He said, "Come unto Me
    all who are weary
    and I will give you rest."
(Chorus again)

76
His Love Is Strong

by Joel Lindsey and Regie Hamm

1. So many mountains
        that we try to climb,
   So many places
        where we fall behind.
   Deep in the struggle
        just to find our way,
   We lose the heart,
        we lose the faith.
   Sometimes this life
        can tear your world apart,

Chorus:
You've got to remember.
    His love is strong enough
    to win the fight.
His love is strong
    and good and right.
When the heart gets weak
    and the road gets long,
His love is strong.
    His love is strong.

2. Within the wonder of a baby's cry,
   And in the thunder
       of a midnight sky,
   Is something stronger
       than the heart of steel.
   It's a power
       you can touch and feel.
   So when you're thinkin'
       all your hope is gone,
(Chorus again)

77
I Build My Life on You

Words by Ken Bible
Music by Randall Dennis

1. On You, O Lord, On You, O Lord,
       I build my life on You.
   You speak to me; I listen, Lord,
       for all that You'd have me do.
   As step by step You lead me on,
       In faith I'll follow through.
   On You, O Lord, On You, O Lord,
       I build my life on You.

2. In You, O Lord, In You, O Lord,
       I live this day in You.
   You're with me now; I worship You
       in spirit and in truth.
   My Prince of Peace, Almighty God,
       With all Your love in view,
   In You, O Lord, In You, O Lord,
       I live this day in You.

78
My Turn Now

*by Steven Curtis Chapman
and Brent Lamb*

Chorus:
Well, it's my turn now.
Well, it's my turn now,
    my turn to give my life away.

Well, it's my turn now.
Well, it's my turn now,
    my turn to give my life away.

Verse:
My turn to say I love Him,
My turn to let Him know
My life is His, so where He leads me—
That's where I will go.
(Chorus again)

79
Hosanna

by Cathy Jeffers Risse

Hosanna, hosanna,
    hosanna to the King!
Exalt Him and worship Him—
    Lord of everything!
Almighty Defender—
    His banner goes before.
Sing your praises to the King of Kings
    and Lord, the Lord of Lords.

80
Lifting Up My Voice

by Dan Whittemore

Jesus, I bow my heart before You,
In worship, lifting up my voice—
Lifting up my voice in honor,
Lifting up my voice in praise,
Lifting up my voice in worship to You.

81
God Is in Control

by Twila Paris

This is no time for fear.
This is a time for faith
    and determination.
Don't lose the vision here,
    carried away by emotion.
Hold on to all
    that you hide in your heart.
There is one thing
    that has always been true.
It holds the world together.

Chorus:
God is in control.
We believe that His children
    will not be forsaken.
God is in control.
We will choose to remember
    and never be shaken.
There is no power above
    or beside Him, we know.
Oh, God is in control.
Oh, God is in control.

82
King Jesus Is All

Author unknown
Arr. by Steven V. Taylor

King Jesus is all,
    (King Jesus is all,)
My all in all,
    (my all in all,)
And I know He'll answer
    (I know He'll answer)
Me when I call.
    (me when I call.)
Walkin' by His side,
    (Walkin' by His side,)

I'm satisfied.
    (I'm satisfied.)
King Jesus is all,
    (King Jesus is all,)
My all in all.
    (my all in all.)

Well, I went out to meet the Lord,
    oh, yeah!
I got down on my knees,
    uh, huh.
I said my very first prayer;
You know, the Holy Ghost
    met me there.
Well, I stepped on the Rock;
    the Rock was sound.
Oh, the love of God
    came a-tumblin' down.
The reason I know
    that He saved my soul is–
I dug down deep
    and I found pure gold.
(Back to the beginning)

83
I Love You, O My Lord

by Dan Whittemore

1. I love You, O my Lord;
   I love You, O my Lord,
   My Rock, my Savior, my Deliverer–
   I love You, O my Lord.
   I love You, O my Lord.

2. You save me when I call;
   You save me when I call.
   There is no triumph for my enemy–
   I love You, O my Lord.
   I love You, O my Lord.

3. Who keeps the lamplight burning?
   Who turns the dark away?
   Who lifts my spirit when I sorrow?
   I love You, O my Lord.
   I love You, O my Lord.

4. I love you, O my Lord;
   I love You, O my Lord.
   O You are worthy of all praises–
   I love You, O my Lord.
   I love You, O my Lord.

84
We Are the Light

by Tom McLain

Chorus:
We are the light of the world;
We are the salt of the earth.
We are to spread the light;
We are to do what's right.
We are the light of the world.

1. Loving, caring,
      sharing from the Father;
   His love, His life,
      share with one another.
(Chorus again)

2. He knows your heart;
      He is ever faithful.
   His love, His life
      make me ever grateful.
(Chorus again)

We are the light of the world.

85
Carry the Torch

by David Baroni
and Lynn Keesecker

We will carry the torch,
   we will lift high the flame,
We will march through the darkness
   with the light of His name

Until the glory of God
   is seen by the world.
We will carry the torch of the Lord.
(Sing again)

we will carry the torch of the Lord.

86
Hidden Treasure

Words by Ken Bible
Music by Randall Dennis

1. With my eyes fixed on my Father,
      I will look to Him alone.
   He is wisdom, He is strength,
         And I'm always near His
         throne.
   I will trust Him in my weakness,
      I will bring Him all my sin;
   I will love with joy and freedom–
      He is God, and God within.

Chorus:
I found a hidden treasure
   Others cannot see;
A hidden treasure;
   God alive in me.
Since He brought His kingdom in,
   I'm living in and unto Him.
I found a hidden treasure:
   God alive in me.

2. Whether prayer or selfdenial,
      Loving act or gentle word,
   Each is worship, each a gift
      Offered only to my Lord.
   When my worries rise before me,
      I remember that I'm His.
   I can rest in His abundance,
      And rejoice in who He is.
(Chorus again)

87
Shoes

Words by Nan Allen
Music by Dennis Allen

1. Whenever I feel my faith is strong,
   It's cause I've got my armor on.
   Whenever I feel my faith is weak,
   I start by lookin' down at the soles
     of my feet!

Chorus:
I need to put on my shoes,
  my gospel shoes,
And walk around
  with the gospel news
And the power flows
  from my head to my toes
When I put on my gospel shoes.

2. With a helmet and sword
     and a righteous vest,
   I still don't feel I'm fully dressed.
   I need a shield of faith
     and a belt of truth,
   But there's one more thing,
     I gotta have my shoes!
   (Chorus again)

Be ready, stand your ground.
Put on the full armor of God.
Be ready, stand your ground.
Stand firm. *Just do it!*
(Chorus again)

88
Facts Are Facts

by Steven Curtis Chapman

1. I don't wanna take up
     anybody's time,
   Just givin' my opinion
     with a rhythm
     and a clever rhyme.
   I don't want these words
     to sound like I think I've got it
     all figured out.

There are a few things I can say
  I know without a doubt:

Chorus:
I know there's a God
  who knows my name
And a Son who died
  to take the blame.
I believe Jesus is comin' back,
'Cause promises are promises
  and facts are facts! Yeah!
Promises are promises
  and facts are facts!

2. These days some say
     there's no one way to believe.
   Just keep it loose; you're free to
     choose.
     There's no absolute; it's all
     relative, you see!
   So I'm callin' all defenders
     of the truth to live a life that
     spells out God's world view.
   Let these words be heard
     in everything you say and do:
   (Chorus again)

And I believe Jesus,
He's comin' back!

Chorus:
I know there's a God
  who knows my name
And a Son who died
  to take the blame.
I believe Jesus is comin' back,
'Cause promises are promises
  and facts are facts!

I know there's a God
  who knows my name
And a Son who died
  to take the blame.
I believe Jesus is comin' back,
'Cause promises are promises
  and facts are facts! Yeah!
Promises are promises
  and facts are facts!
Promises are promises
  and facts are facts!

89
May Your Presence Purify My Heart

Words by Ken Bible
Music by Stephen V. Taylor

Father, Father, Jesus, Lord Jesus,
    Spirit most holy, You are here.
May Your presence purify my heart
    As my spirit bows to all You are.
Plant Your holy love in every part.
    May Your presence
    purify my heart.
Father, Father, Jesus, Lord Jesus,
    Spirit most holy, You are here.

90
Leaning on the Everlasting Arms

Words by Elisha Hoffman
Music by Anthony Showalter
Arr. by Dennis Allen

1. What a fellowship,
        what a joy divine,
    Leaning on the everlasting arms.
    What a blessedness,
        what a peace is mine,
    Leaning on the everlasting arms.

Chorus:
Leaning, leaning,
    safe and secure from all alarms,
Leaning, leaning,
    leaning on the everlasting arms.

2. Oh, how sweet to walk
        in this pilgrim way,
    Leaning on the everlasting arms.
    Oh, how bright the path
        grows from day to day,
    Leaning on the everlasting arms.

Leaning, leaning,
    safe and secure from all alarms,
Leaning, leaning,
    leaning on the everlasting arms.

91
Great Is the Lord

by Patrick Henderson

Great is the Lord;
He is great to be praised
    in the mountain of His holiness.
Great is the Lord;
He is great to be praised
    in the mountain of His holiness.

92
Clap Your Hands

by Danny Hamilton

Clap your hands
    all ye people.
Shout it to the Lord
    with the voice triumphant.
Clap your hands,
    clap your hands.
Praise Him with the sound
    of the voice and trumpet.

Clap your hands,
    clap your hands.
Shout it from the top
    of the tallest mountain.
Clap your hands,
    clap your hands   And praise
the Lord.

93
Higher Ground

Words by Johnson Oatman, Jr.
Music by Dennis Allen

1. I'm pressing on the upward way;
     (I'm pressing on
     the upward way;)
   New heights I'm gaining
   every day.
     (New heights I'm gaining
     every day.)
   Still praying as I'm onward bound,
     (Still praying as
     I'm onward bound,)
   "Lord, plant my feet
   on higher ground."
     ("Lord, plant my feet
     on higher ground.")

Chorus:
Lord, lift me up and let me stand,
By faith, on heaven's tableland,
A higher plane than I have found.
Lord, plant my feet on higher ground,
   on higher ground.

2. I want to live above the world,
     (I want to live
     above the world,)
   Though Satan's darts
   at me are hurled.
     (Though Satan's darts
     at me are hurled.)
   For faith has caught
   the joyful sound,
     (For faith has caught
     the joyful sound,)
   The song of saints
   on higher ground.
     (The song of saints
     on higher ground.)

Lord, lift me up and let me stand,
By faith, on heaven's tableland,
A higher plane than I have found.
Lord, plant my feet on higher ground,
   on higher ground.

94
Seek Ye First

by Karen Lafferty

1. Seek ye first the kingdom of God
     and His righteousness,
   And all these things
     shall be added unto you.
   Allelu, alleluia.

2. Man shall not live by bread alone,
     but by every word
   That proceeds
     from the mouth of God.
   Allelu, alleluia.

3. Ask, and it shall be given unto you;
     seek and ye shall find.
   Knock, and the door
     shall be opened unto you.
   Allelu, alleluia.

4. Seek ye first the kingdom of God
     and His righteousness,
   And all these things
     shall be added unto you.
   Allelu, alleluia.

95
Above All Else

by Kirk & Deby Dearman

You are exalted,
   Lord, above all else;
We place You at the highest place
   above all else.
Right now where we stand and
   everywhere we go,
We place You at the highest place
   so the world will know:

You are a Mighty Warrior
   dressed in armor of light,

Crushing the deeds of darkness,
lead us on in the fight.
Through the blood of Jesus,
victorious we stand;
We place You at the highest place
above all else in this land.

96
Thy Word

*by Amy Grant and
Michael W. Smith*

Thy Word is a lamp unto my feet
and a light unto my path.
Thy Word is a lamp unto my feet
and a light unto my path.

97
Joy!

*Words by George W. Cook
Music by Amy Grant*

1. I got the joy, (joy)
joy, (joy) joy, (joy)
I got the joy, (joy)
joy, (joy) joy, (joy)
I got the joy, (joy) joy, (joy) joy,

Chorus:
Two, three, four!
Down in my heart,
Down in my heart,
Down in my heart to stay,
Down in my heart to stay!

2. I got the love, (love)
love, (love), love, (love)
I got the love, (love)
love, (love), love, (love)

I got the love, (love)
love, (love) love,

Two, three, four!
Down in my heart,
Down in my heart,
Down in my heart to stay,
Down in my heart to stay!

98
I Will Call upon the Lord

*Words adapted by Michael O'Shields
Music by Michael O'Shields*

I will call upon the Lord
(I will call upon the Lord)
who is worthy to be praised.
(who is worthy to be praised.)
So shall I be saved from my enemies.
(So shall I be saved
from my enemies.)
I will call upon the Lord.

The Lord liveth,
and blessed be the Rock,
And let the God of my salvation
be exalted.
The Lord liveth,
and blessed be the Rock,
And let the God of my salvation
be exalted.

The Lord liveth,
and blessed be the Rock,
And let the God of my salvation
be exalted.
The Lord liveth,
and blessed be the Rock,
And let the God of my salvation
be exalted.

99
Build a Bridge

by Dennis and Nan Allen

1. There was a gulf that separated us
From the perfect heart of God.
But with the gift of His own Son,
God made the way for us to cross.
Now because we know the way
We can't be silent for one more
day.

Chorus:
Build a bridge
   reaching out the hand of Christ.
Join together,
   all as one, side by side.
We will tell all the world
   that in Jesus Christ alone
   there is hope.
Join together, reaching out,
build a bridge,
Build a bridge.

2. There is one thing that has united
us,
We have a bond of faith.
And together we can build
A bridge His love thro' us creates.
Then we'll earn the right to share
With a world that needs to hear.
(Chorus again)

We are His hands to the needy.
We are His voice to the lost.
We can take the heart of God
   to the world.
(Chorus again)

Build a bridge, (build a bridge)
Build a bridge, (build a bridge)
Build a bridge.

Songs for Youth

ALPHABETICAL INDEX